Planets for Kids

FUN FACTS ABOUT OUR SOLAR SYSTEM

Preeti Singh

Sun

Mercury

Venus

Earth

Mars

Asteroid belt

Jupiter

Saturn

Uranus

The solar system is made up of the Sun and the eight planets. It also includes many small objects such as dwarf planets, asteroids, comets and meteoroids.

Neptune

The planets and all objects orbit around the Sun.
(Orbit means to circle around)

Rocky planets

Mercury

Venus

Earth

Mars

Mercury, Venus, Earth and Mars are made up of rocks and are known as rocky planets.

Gas planets

Saturn

Neptune

Jupiter

Uranus

Jupiter, Saturn, Uranus and Neptune are made up of gas and are known as gas planets.

All gas planets have rings, but Saturn has the most visible ones.

Sun is the largest object in our solar system.

It is a very bright star that gives heat and light.

Sun supports life on Earth.

Sun

It is the center of our solar system.

More than a million Earth's can fit inside the Sun - it is huge!

Many craters cover Mercury's surface.

It has no Moons.

It is the smallest planet in our solar system.

Mercury
It is the 1st planet from the Sun.

Mercury is the fastest to orbit around the Sun as it is closest to the Sun.

Venus is often called "Earth's twin" because it is almost the same size as Earth.

Venus rotates from east to west, which is the oppposite direction from most planets.

When viewed from Earth, it is the 2nd brightest object in the sky after Moon.

Venus

It is the 2nd planet from the Sun.

It has no Moons.

Venus is the hottest planet because it is always covered with thick yellow clouds which trap the Sun's heat.

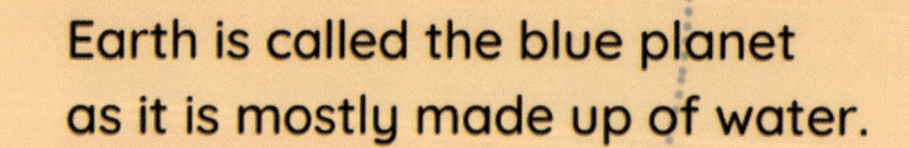

Earth is called the blue planet
as it is mostly made up of water.

It was formed 4.5 billion years ago.

It has one Moon.

Moon is the brightest object that we can
see in the sky from Earth.
Venus and Jupiter come next.

Earth

It is the 3rd planet from the Sun.

Earth is the only planet where life exists. Plants, animals, humans and many life forms live on Earth.

Mars is called the red planet because it's surface is covered with red colored rusty dust.

It has two small Moons.

Mars
It is the 4th planet from the Sun.

Mars has many mountains, canyons and deep valleys. The largest mountain in the solar system is on Mars.

Jupiter is a gas planet and it is also the biggest planet in our solar system. So it is also called the gas giant.

It has the most Moons in our solar system.

When viewed from Earth, It is the 3rd biggest object in the sky after Moon and Venus.

Jupiter

It is the 5th planet from the Sun.

Jupiter has the famous Great Red Spot. This is a storm that has been around for more than 300 years!

Saturn is famous for its big beautiful rings.
The rings are made up of dust and ice.

It has many moons.

Saturn
It is the 6th planet from the Sun.

Saturn is the 2nd largest planet in the solar system. It is also a gas giant.

Uranus is one of the two ice giants.
It is very cold there.

It is the 3rd largest planet in the solar system and has many moons.

Just like Venus, Uranus also rotates from east to west.

Uranus

It is the 7th planet from the Sun.

Uranus is the only planet that rotates sideways.

Neptune is the 2nd ice giant after Uranus.

It is a very dark and windy planet.

Neptune
It is the 8th planet from the Sun.

Neptune is the furthest planet from the Sun and hence it is also the coldest planet.

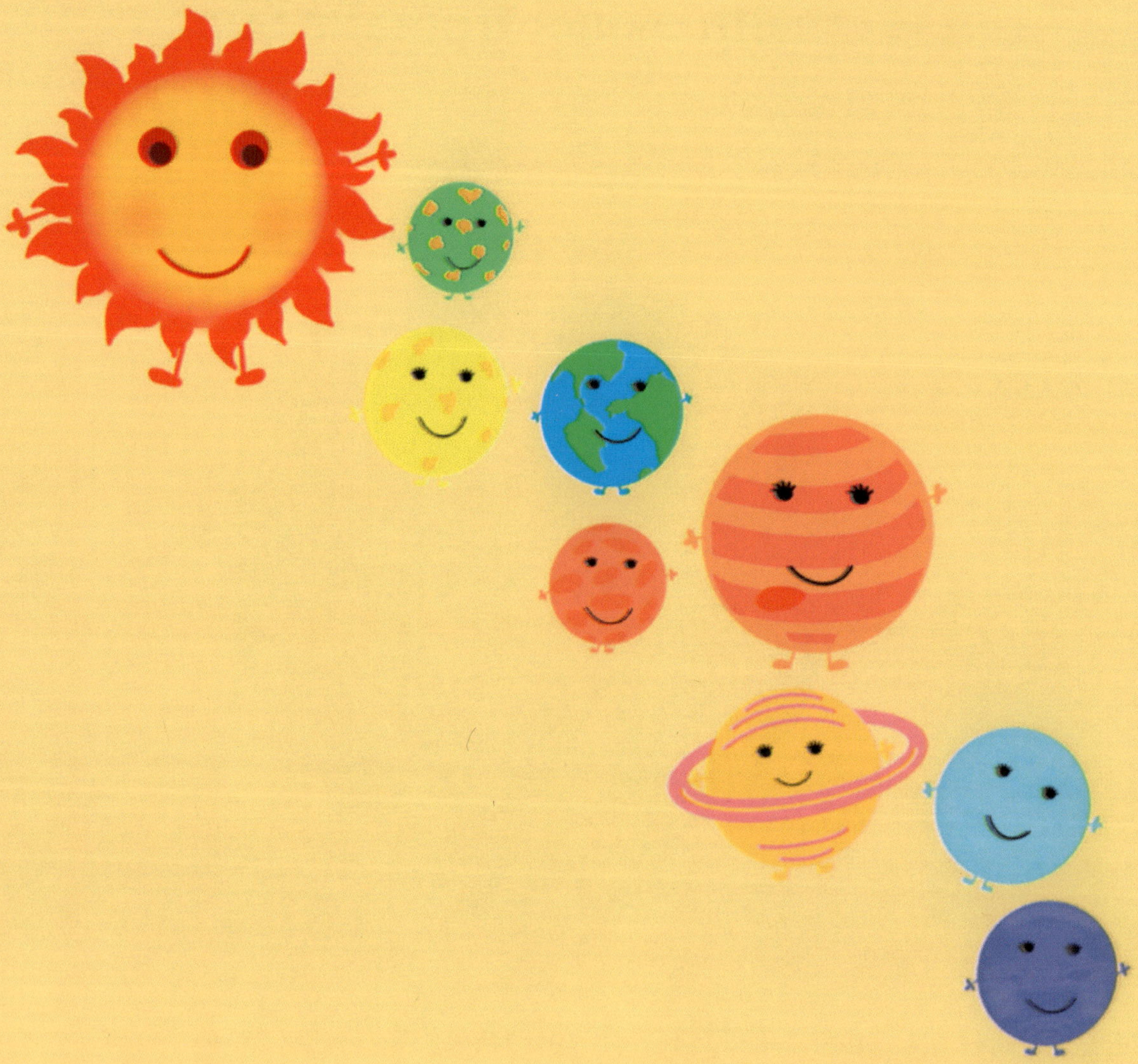

Fun quiz for kids

1. How many planets are there in our solar system?
2. Which planet is the smallest?
3. Which planet is the furthest from the Sun?
4. Which planet is called the "Red planet"?
5. Which planet has the most visible rings?
6. Which is the only planet that has life on it?
7. Which planet is the hottest?
8. Which planet is the closest to the Sun?
9. Which is the biggest planet?
10. Which planet spins sideways?

Answers:
1. Eight, 2. Mercury, 3. Neptune, 4. Mars, 5. Saturn,
6. Earth, 7. Venus, 8. Mercury, 9. Jupiter 10. Uranus

Solar System Bookmarks
Cut along the colored edges

Sun

Mercury

Venus

Earth

Mars

Jupiter

Saturn

Uranus

Neptune

Solar System

Sun

Mercury

Venus

Earth

Mars

Jupiter

Saturn

Uranus

Neptune

Solar System

Sun

Mercury

Venus

Earth

Mars

Jupiter

Saturn

Uranus

Neptune

Solar System

If you wish to tear the page completely, please do so at the dotted line as shown.

Sun & planets craft

Sun

1. Cut along the sides of the Sun and the planets. 2. Paste them on a round piece of cardboard. 3. Attach them to a craft stick. 4. Write the names of each planet on the craft stick. 5. Arrange them in order around the Sun.

If you wish to tear the page completely, please do so at the dotted line as shown.

Mercury

Venus

Earth

Mars

Planets cutouts

Jupiter

Saturn

Uranus

Neptune

Planets cutouts

For Ahaan, my shining star forever.

Illustrations copyright © 2021 Preeti Singh
Designed & Illustrated by: Preeti Singh

All rights reserved. No part of this book may be reproduced or used in any manner without the prior written permission of the copyright owner, except for the use of brief quotations in a book review.

For information contact: psbookinfo@gmail.com

ISBN: 9798596468526
Independently published

Printed in Great Britain
by Amazon